Wealth Beyond the Number

WEALTH BEYOND THE NUMBER

Defining Enough in an Age of Endless Accumulation

Sreedhar K

First published 2026.

ISBN: 978-93-5786-824-2

Disclaimer

This book is intended for informational and educational purposes only. It does not constitute financial, investment, legal, or professional advice of any kind. The frameworks, strategies, and examples presented are illustrative and general in nature. Individual financial circumstances vary significantly. Readers are strongly advised to consult qualified financial advisors, legal professionals, and other relevant experts before making any financial or investment decisions. The author and publisher accept no liability for any loss or damage arising from reliance on the contents of this book.

In loving memory of my Father and Mother

who taught me to spread the blanket according to its size,

and that dignity is the greatest asset one can own.

CONTENT

AUTHOR'S NOTE

A word before we begin

This book began as an attempt to answer a question I had been carrying for years without naming it.

I had spent over three decades in corporate leadership; navigating strategy, transformation, and the relentless pressure of performance across global organisations. I was reasonably good at the work. I was less good at stopping to ask what the work was for.

When I stepped away from a full-time corporate role closer to 60, I expected relief. What arrived instead was a more unsettling clarity: the frameworks I had used to build a career had almost nothing to say about what to do once the career had served its purpose. The financial plans were in order. The question of meaning was not.

The answer, or the beginning of one, came from going back to our roots. Not as an act of nostalgia, but as a practical search. The ancient Indian philosophical tradition, I found, had spent considerable time on the exact question that modern planning skips: not how much, but what for. Not how to grow, but when growing has served its purpose.

Two experiences shaped the emotional texture of this book more than any framework.

The first was my father. He retired on a modest pension when I was twenty-one, still in university. What I remember is not scarcity but discipline; a life adjusted to means rather than means stretched to desire. He left behind savings he never spent. His life was the first lesson in the Enough-Point, given without a single word about money.

The second was my mother's illness in her later years. By then I had resources my father never had; access, options, the full architecture of Artha. And yet I learned, in those months, the precise boundary of what wealth can and cannot do. That experience is in this book, briefly but honestly.

I have also drawn on what I observed in three decades alongside exceptional leaders; talented, disciplined people who had mastered accumulation and found, at the summit, that they had not been asked the right questions on the way up.

This book is for them. It is for anyone who has built well and is now asking what to build towards. It is not a spiritual text. It is not a financial planning manual. It sits between those two things, which is where I believe the most important questions about money actually live.

A note on how to read it: the chapters are sequential and build on each other. Chapter 1 gives you the full landscape of wealth. Chapters 2 and 3 diagnose the problem and give you the primary tool. Chapters 4 and 5 build the architecture. Chapter 6 describes what changes when the architecture is in place. If you are in a hurry, read the Introduction and Chapter 3 first; they contain the central question and the central tool. Then come back to the rest.

> *These are not borrowed insights. They are earned ones.*

Sreedhar K

March 2026

Yoga is the journey of the self,
through the self, to the self.

— Bhagavad Gita, VI.20

INTRODUCTION

The Question Nobody Asks

How thirty years of answers left the most important question unanswered

I have sat in a great many planning sessions over the course of my career. Boardrooms. Offsite strategy retreats. Year-end reviews where we laid out projections, mapped scenarios, and drew confident lines on charts pointing upward and to the right. I was good at those sessions. I knew how to ask the right questions, challenge the assumptions, and leave with a plan that everyone felt anchored to.

It took me a long time to notice that there was one question nobody ever asked. Not in the boardrooms. Not in the financial planning meetings I attended for myself. Not in the leadership conversations where we talked endlessly about growth, scale, and the next horizon.

> *What is this all actually for?*

I spent over thirty years in corporate leadership; bridging strategy and execution, leading transformations, building teams across global organisations. I understood the what and the how with reasonable competence. But the why had a habit of going quietly unanswered, buried under the urgency of whatever came next.

When I stepped away to found an independent advisory practice, I finally had the stillness to sit with that question. The answer did not come from a financial planner or a retirement calculator. It came from going back to our roots; to Vedic philosophy, to the ancient concept of the Purusharthas, to a body of wisdom that treats wealth not as a destination but as one instrument in a larger life.

That return to roots gave me something that three decades of excellent planning had not: a framework for sufficiency. Not just how much to save, but what the saving was for. Not just how to grow, but when growing had served its purpose. Not just how to succeed, but what success meant at the level of a whole life.

What This Book Is, and Is Not

This is not another retirement planning book. It is for the person who has read those books, followed the advice, built the spreadsheets, and still feels that something essential is missing. The numbers are in order. The anxiety is not.

The Vedic frameworks here, the Ashta Lakshmi, the Purusharthas, the concept of Kama, are treated as functional tools, not as spiritual prescriptions. They have survived thousands of years because they describe human nature accurately and answer questions that modern financial theory simply does not ask.

What this book offers is a bridge. Ancient wisdom on one side. Modern financial architecture on the other. The bridge is the question that connects them: not how much do I have, but what is actually enough?

✦ Before You Begin

1. Across the eight dimensions of wealth, financial, physical, relational, intellectual, social, spiritual, psychological, and service, where are you genuinely rich, and where are you quietly impoverished?
2. When did you last feel that what you had was sufficient? What changed?
3. Is your current definition of 'enough' your own, or did you inherit it from the environment around you?

One who sees inaction in action, and action in inaction, is wise among men.

— Bhagavad Gita, IV.18

CHAPTER 1

What Is Wealth, Really?

The Ashta Lakshmi: Eight Dimensions of Prosperity

We live in a world obsessed with a singular, narrow definition of success: the size of our bank accounts and the material wealth we have accumulated. We chase it at the expense of our purpose, our relationships, and our health, often sacrificing everything to get ahead. I have seen many who scale the peaks of material success, only to realise at the summit that they have conquered the wrong mountain. They stand triumphant, yet profoundly poor.

The poverty I am describing is not financial. It is the poverty of a life optimised for one dimension at the cost of seven others.

My First Lesson in Wealth

When my father retired from Indian railway service, I was barely twenty-one and still in university. His pension was modest. There was no dramatic fall; just a narrowing of possibilities. What I remember most from those years was not scarcity. It was discipline.

He never chased luxuries on borrowed money. No loans for status. No EMIs for appearance. If something could not be paid for from what was already earned, it waited. He did leave behind savings; carefully accumulated from that modest pension. But he did not enjoy them in any visible way. No indulgences deferred to retirement. No late-life upgrades.

What he practised instead was sufficiency. A life adjusted to means, not means stretched to match desire. We learned early to spread the blanket according to its size. If your legs extended beyond it, you changed your posture; not the blanket.

> *It took me decades to realise that this was my first lesson in wealth. Not accumulation. Not growth curves. Not optimisation. Proportion. Dignity within limits. A quiet refusal to mortgage tomorrow's peace for today's appearance.*

The Ashta Lakshmi gave me the language for what I had witnessed in that household without being able to name it. By conventional measures, my father was modest in Dhana Lakshmi. Yet he was deeply wealthy in many of the other dimensions; in his integrity, his relationships, his health, his quiet courage, his presence, his sense of purpose. The dimension society measures most loudly happened to be the one that mattered least in the way he lived.

The Illusion of 'Only Money'

Money is a vital tool; it provides security, comfort, and the freedom to make choices. But money alone cannot buy the things that make a life feel worth living. In thirty years working alongside highly successful people, I observed four things that money, beyond a threshold, consistently failed to provide.

Meaning and Purpose

A high net worth does not equate to a high sense of purpose. I have watched leaders at the peak of their careers describe a quiet sense of futility they could not name to their colleagues. The singular zeal to accumulate had crowded out the question of what the accumulation was for.

Vitality

You cannot trade gold for a single day of lost health. The habits sacrificed to the demands of the career, sleep, exercise, nutrition, stress management, are presented as temporary compromises. They rarely are. At sixty, having trained for long-distance triathlons, I have learned that vitality is not recoverable on demand. It is built daily, or it diminishes gradually.

Presence

Money can buy a house, but not the moments you cherish inside it. The executive who funds the family holiday but spends it on the phone has purchased the location but missed the experience. Presence cannot be delegated or deferred without cost.

Peace

External riches often bring internal anxiety. The fear of loss, of the portfolio, the position, the reputation, can consume far more of a person's inner life than the pleasure of possession ever produced.

> *Real wealth is not the string of zeros preceded by an integer. It is a portfolio of prosperity with eight diverse assets; drawn from the ancient Vedic concept of Ashta Lakshmi.*

The Eight Forms of Wealth

1. Adi Lakshmi : Spiritual Wealth

Internal strength and source. The daily habit of self-mastery and connection with your deeper self. In practice: twenty minutes of quiet before the world makes its demands. Whether through meditation, prayer, or stillness; this internal anchor is not spiritual decoration. It is operational infrastructure.

2. Dhana Lakshmi : Financial Wealth

Fuel for freedom; not greed. Having enough resources to say no to misalignment and yes to purpose. Financial wealth, properly understood, is about options: the freedom to make decisions based on purpose rather than desperation.

3. Dhanya Lakshmi : Health Wealth

Our energy levels, physical capacity, and longevity. A healthy person has a thousand wishes; a sick person has only one. Health is the wealth that makes all other pursuits possible. The investment compounds over decades, and unlike financial capital, it cannot be borrowed against or recovered through windfall.

4. Gaja Lakshmi : Social Wealth

Your network and your reputation. True social wealth reveals itself in difficult times; who answers when you call, who offers guidance without judgment. Built slowly, through authenticity and generosity, without a scorecard.

5. Santana Lakshmi : Relational Wealth

The quality of your closest relationships and the legacy created within them. The 10,000 Dinners Question: if you only had a limited number of meals left with the people you love, how would you treat this one? My father's relational wealth was extraordinary; the consistency of his presence, the quality of his attention, the uncomplicated warmth extended without condition.

6. Dhairya Lakshmi : Courage Wealth

The courage to take risks, fail forward, and remain patient when results do not arrive immediately. This dimension allows reinvention at any stage of life. Every challenge navigated with valour builds this reserve. Every challenge avoided depletes it.

7. Vidya Lakshmi : Intellectual Wealth

The continuous pursuit of mastery and the curiosity that keeps the mind alive. The 60-minute masterwork: one hour of focused, phone-free deep work each day on the thing that matters most to your craft. Mastery happens in sustained focus, not fragmented attention.

8. Vijaya Lakshmi : Impact Wealth

The victory of a life lived for something larger than yourself. Measured not in accolades but in lives touched, knowledge shared, and positive change catalysed. The Live-to-Give habit: one small act of genuine service each day reminds you that you are a contributor to the world, not merely a beneficiary.

The Honest Audit

Before moving forward, score yourself honestly across all eight dimensions.

Dimension	**Modern Lens**	**Your Score (1–10)**
Adi Lakshmi	Spiritual / Internal Wealth	___
Dhana Lakshmi	Financial Wealth	___
Dhanya Lakshmi	Health Wealth	___
Gaja Lakshmi	Social Wealth	___
Santana Lakshmi	Relational / Family Wealth	___
Dhairya Lakshmi	Psychological / Courage Wealth	___

Dimension	Modern Lens	Your Score (1–10)
Vidya Lakshmi	Intellectual Wealth	___
Vijaya Lakshmi	Impact / Service Wealth	___

Where is the largest gap? The rest of this book is about closing those gaps; not by accumulating more, but by distributing your attention more honestly across the full portfolio of a wealthy life.

Practising the Ashta Lakshmi : Daily Architecture

Knowing the eight dimensions is the map. The practices below are the terrain. Even small, consistent actions across all eight dimensions compound into a life that feels genuinely wealthy; not occasionally, but as a baseline.

Dimension	Core Practice	What It Builds
Adi Lakshmi Spiritual	20 minutes of stillness before the world makes demands; meditation, journalling, or quiet reflection	*Internal anchor; the day begins from intention, not reaction*
Dhana Lakshmi Financial	Monthly Kama filter review: examine every recurring expenditure; confirm the architecture is being funded	*Clarity on what money is for; reduces financial anxiety at source*

Dimension	Core Practice	What It Builds
Dhanya Lakshmi Health	Protect sleep, daily movement, and one meal eaten without distraction; the endurance athlete's non-negotiables	*Energy compounds over decades; vitality cannot be borrowed from the future*
Gaja Lakshmi Social	One genuine act of generosity or mentorship per week; no scorecard, no expectation of return	*A network built on trust rather than transaction; it reveals itself in difficult times*
Santana Lakshmi Relational	The 10,000 Dinners practice: one meal per week fully present; phone away, attention given without condition	*Relational wealth compounds exactly as financial wealth does; every present dinner is an investment*

Dimension	Core Practice	What It Builds
Dhairya Lakshmi Courage	One act of honest discomfort per month; a difficult conversation, a creative risk, a decision deferred too long	*Courage is a practised capacity; each avoided challenge quietly erodes it*
Vidya Lakshmi Intellectual	The 60-minute masterwork: one hour of deep, distraction-free work each day on the thing that matters most to your craft	*Mastery is built in sustained focus; fragmented attention produces volume without depth*

Dimension	Core Practice	What It Builds
Vijaya Lakshmi Impact	The Live-to-Give habit: one act of genuine service daily; teaching, contributing, solving a problem that is not your own	*A life organised around contribution rather than accumulation; purpose replaces the treadmill*

The table does not demand perfection across all eight simultaneously. It asks for intention. A single practice per dimension, maintained honestly, produces more genuine wealth than any single-axis strategy ever will.

Understanding the eight dimensions is clarifying. But clarity alone does not produce change. Most people do not neglect the other dimensions because they reject them. They neglect them because something more subtle is at work; a mechanism that quietly overrides the values they already hold.

✦ Chapter 1 Reflection

1. Complete the scoring grid above honestly. Where is your largest gap between financial wealth and the rest?
2. Which dimension, if genuinely improved, would most change your daily experience?
3. What have you sacrificed in one dimension to advance another, and was that trade conscious, or did it accumulate without decision?

For the uncontrolled, there is no wisdom, and for the uncontrolled there is no concentration; and for him without concentration, there is no peace; and for the unpeaceful, how can there be happiness?

— Bhagavad Gita, II.66

CHAPTER 2

The Trap

Why the Finish Line Keeps Moving?

There is a particular kind of fatigue that comes not from overwork but from over-striving. The exhaustion of the person who has achieved what they set out to achieve, and found themselves reaching for the next thing before the satisfaction of the last has even settled. I have watched it in boardrooms across three decades. I have seen it in the eyes of leaders who, by every external measure, had everything, and who could not quite explain why that did not feel like enough.

This is not a character flaw. It is a mechanism. And until you understand the mechanism, you cannot escape it.

The Lesson of Impermanence

My father spent his life stretching modest earnings across education, responsibility, and dignity. He saved what he could; never dramatically, but consistently. When he passed, the savings remained. He did not take them with him.

What he left instead was something more unsettling than grief: the realisation that the accumulation we exhaust ourselves protecting has a time horizon we do not control.

> *That was the first time I understood, not intellectually, but viscerally, that the finish line keeps moving until life quietly ends the race. The treadmill does not stop on its own. If we do not define enough, time will define it for us.*

His savings sat in a bank account, carefully preserved from a life of careful restraint. He had been too disciplined to spend them. Too conditioned by scarcity to permit himself the pleasures they might have funded. The lesson was not that he had failed. It was that sufficiency without the courage to actually live from it is an incomplete discipline.

The Hedonic Treadmill

Psychologists call it hedonic adaptation. The ancient Vedic texts called it Trishna; craving. Human beings have a remarkable capacity to return to a baseline level of satisfaction regardless of what they gain or lose. The promotion that was supposed to change everything becomes the new normal within months. The house that felt like arrival becomes simply where you live.

The treadmill metaphor is apt. You can run very fast on it. You can exhaust yourself on it. But you do not actually go anywhere. The finish line is not ahead of you. It is built into the machine.

> *We do not have a wealth problem. We have a definition problem. Nobody told us what we were running towards, so we kept running.*

In my corporate years, I watched organisations succumb to the institutional version of this same trap. Targets were set. Targets were met. New targets appeared, calibrated slightly beyond what had just been achieved. We called this ambition. What it often was, in practice, was an absence of intentionality.

Lifestyle Creep: Trishna in a Business Suit

Trishna, the unexamined craving described in the previous section, does not announce itself as craving. In financial life it arrives as lifestyle creep: expenses that expand quietly to match income, each individual escalation feeling justified, the aggregate silently consuming whatever surplus might have funded freedom.

- The subscription that renews automatically and is used perhaps twice a month.
- The upgrade that costs 40% more and delivers 10% more actual satisfaction.

- The renovation triggered not by necessity but by a neighbour's recently renovated kitchen.
- The car replaced three years before it needed replacing because the new model was available.

None of these, individually, is catastrophic. Together, they represent years of compounded freedom deferred.

The Comparison Trap

The treadmill accelerates when powered by comparison. Our nervous systems were calibrated in small communities where relative position mattered. That calibration has not updated to account for a world where we compare ourselves to a global highlight reel of selective achievement. We see the outcome, never the cost, the compromise, or the private anxiety that often accompanies it.

> *I have seen many who scale the peaks of material success, only to realise at the summit that they have conquered the wrong mountain. They stand triumphant, yet profoundly poor.*

Why High-Achievers Are Most Vulnerable

The trap is most dangerous for those most competent at escaping it. High-achievers are disproportionately vulnerable because success keeps rewarding the very behaviour that causes the problem. The drive, the discipline, the refusal to accept current performance as a ceiling; these produced the results. They also make it almost impossible to stop.

The ones who struggled most in their transitions, out of corporate life, toward a second chapter, were often the ones most successful in the first. They had been so well rewarded for striving that they had never developed a language for sufficiency. The question 'what is enough?' felt like surrender. It was not. It was the most sophisticated strategic question available to them.

The Moving Goalpost: One More Year

There is a specific variant of the treadmill that deserves its own name. It is the 'one more year' rationalisation; the private agreement made with oneself that the transition will happen, but not yet. One more bonus cycle. One more promotion. One more milestone that will, finally, make the number feel secure enough to stop.

The mechanism is familiar to anyone who has used it. The year ends. The bonus arrives. The number has moved, and so has the goalpost. The next threshold appears with its own compelling logic: the market conditions, the children's fees, the project not yet complete, the successor not yet ready. There is always a reason that is true and never a reason that is sufficient. The rationalisation is not dishonest. It is the Trishna described in Chapter 3 in detail, wearing the clothing of prudence.

What makes this variant particularly difficult is that it is socially rewarded. Nobody questions the person who says they are staying one more year to be responsible. Nobody challenges the logic of one more bonus. The trap is legitimised by the very environment that created it. The corporate world speaks fluently about growth and almost never about sufficiency. In that context, defining enough looks like giving up, when in fact it is the most sophisticated act of planning available.

> *The goalpost does not move because you failed to reach it. It moves because nobody told you it was allowed to stay still.*

✦ Chapter 2 Reflection

1. Where do you notice Trishna operating in your own life; the upgrade, the subscription, the comparison that silently moved your finish line?
2. Which of your current expenses were conscious choices and which were defaults that accumulated without decision?
3. Who are you comparing yourself to, and did you choose that comparison, or did it choose you?

Let right deeds be thy motive,
not the fruit which comes
from them.

— Bhagavad Gita, II.47

CHAPTER 3

The Enough-Point

Kama and the Art of Conscious Desire

Aspiration and Inheritance

As a first-generation corporate professional from a middle-class family, I carried more than my own ambitions. My parents had dreams they had not been able to pursue. Education was their vehicle for me. Achievement was their insurance policy. Success, in those early years, was not just personal; it was generational.

Every promotion was not just mine; it was a validation of the sacrifice that had made it possible. That context made the question of 'enough' genuinely difficult to ask. How do you define sufficiency when the accumulation is partly an act of gratitude, partly a debt you are trying to repay?

> *It took me time to separate aspiration from inheritance. To ask which desires were truly mine and which were expectations absorbed without question. The Enough-Point is not just a financial calculation. It is an act of psychological clarity. It requires you to examine whether the life you are funding is one you consciously chose, or one that arrived with the furniture.*

That examination is uncomfortable. It may reveal that some of what you have been striving for was never yours to begin with. It may also reveal, with surprising clarity, what genuinely matters when you strip away the inherited ambitions and social comparisons. That residue, honest, specific, entirely your own, is where the Enough-Point lives.

Before filling any bucket. Before building any plan. There is a question that must be answered first:

> *What is the minimum expenditure that produces the maximum fulfilment?*

That number, honest, examined, stripped of ego and inherited expectation, is your Enough-Point. It is not the minimum you can endure. It is the optimum you can define. The difference between those two is where genuine freedom lives.

Kama: Not What You Think

Kama is commonly translated as desire, and often dismissed as the dimension of the Purusharthas that sanctions indulgence. This is a misreading. The sages understood that suppressing desire is as dangerous as surrendering to it. What Kama prescribes is neither surrender nor suppression; it is examination. Desire brought consciously into view, tested against the question of what it is actually for, and then either honoured deliberately or released without guilt.

The Four Dimensions of Kama

The Kama filter produces four questions; one for each type of expenditure. The table below applies each question practically. You will notice a column headed 'Bucket 1 Application.' Chapter 4 builds this architecture in full. For now, understand Bucket 1 simply as your safety foundation: the reserve that funds your life for four years without you needing to earn, sell, or worry. Every expense you allow into it should pass the Kama test first. That is the connection between this chapter and the next.

Dimension	The Test	Bucket 1 Application
Bhoga (Enjoyment)	Was this planned and anticipated, or did it appear on the statement as a surprise?	Build a named Experiences line in Bucket 1, holiday, milestone dinner, budgeted in advance, enjoyed without guilt.

Dimension	The Test	Bucket 1 Application
Trishna (Craving)	Does this serve my life or signal my status? If the honest answer is status, it does not belong in the baseline.	Every recurring expense examined annually. If it does not pass the test, it is removed.
Rati (Connection)	Does this expenditure create genuine presence with the people I love, or does it substitute for it?	Fund experiences over objects. Shared meals, family time; these belong.

Dimension	The Test	Bucket 1 Application
Upakarana (Comforts)	Does this support my health, my productivity, or my dignity, or does it merely upgrade my image?	Quality healthcare, reliable vehicle, ergonomic workspace. Upgrade only when function improves.

Bhoga : The Art of Planned Pleasure

Bhoga is the legitimate enjoyment of life's pleasures. The crucial distinction is between planned Bhoga and unplanned expenditure. Planned pleasure; budgeted in advance, anticipated with intention, experienced without guilt; is Bhoga. The impulse purchase decided in the moment is Trishna wearing Bhoga's clothing. The test is simple: did you choose this in advance, or did it choose you?

Trishna : The Discipline of Examination

Every impulse that reaches for the wallet must pass through a single question: is this a genuine need that serves my life, or is this noise, comparison, boredom, habit, or the automated response of a consumer environment designed to generate wants? The filter demands that you know, and that you decide from that knowledge rather than the rationalisation.

Rati : The Wealth of Connection

The most profound human needs are relational rather than material. Financial security itself is an act of relational love; the family freed from financial anxiety is a family that can be more fully present with each other. My father understood this instinctively. His discipline was, in part, an act of protection. That act of love had no receipt attached to it.

Upakarana : The Legitimate Comfort

Comforts that enable a person to live and work with dignity, health, and effectiveness. The

Upakarana test is function versus ego: does this make my life better, or does it make me look better? Upgrade only when function improves, not when ego suggests it.

Cutting Extravagance Without Cutting Life

Applying the Kama filter does not strip pleasure from life. It strips noise. The streaming subscriptions used occasionally. The gym membership that became a direct debit. The business class upgrade on the one-hour flight. None of these is a pleasure; they are habits wearing the clothing of pleasures. Removing them does not diminish quality of life.

> *Cutting extravagance is not austerity. It is clarity. The pleasures that pass the Kama filter are enjoyed more fully, precisely because they were chosen.*

Your Enough-Point

Once the filter has been applied honestly, the number that remains is your Enough-Point baseline; your genuine monthly requirement for a life lived well, not performed impressively. This number is the foundation of everything that follows. It determines the size of your Bucket 1. It is the number after which you are no longer choosing between security and life.

A number without a home, however, is just another anxiety. Knowing what you need is not the same as protecting it. The next question is structural: where does this number live, and what ensures it is always available regardless of what the economy, your employer, or the market decides to do in any given year? That question is what Chapter 4 answers.

> *The Enough-Point tells you what to protect. The architecture tells you how.*

✦ Chapter 3 Reflection

1. Apply the Kama filter to last month's spending. For each significant expenditure: which dimension does it serve?

2. When you strip away inherited expectations and social comparisons, what does your life genuinely need to feel fulfilling?

3. What one expenditure, if eliminated, would you not actually miss, but have never questioned?

Perform your duty equi-poised, abandoning all attachment to success or failure.

— Bhagavad Gita, II.48

CHAPTER 4

The Architecture

Building Your 3-Bucket Life

The Architecture of Endurance

My own career path was not a smooth, uninterrupted climb. There were periods of uncertainty, organisational resets, health challenges that forced me to slow down before I was ready, and reinventions I had not entirely planned for. Training for long-distance triathlons later in life became a metaphor for something I had learned much earlier: you cannot sprint indefinitely.

You need structure. You need pacing. You need reserves built into the design; not as a concession to weakness, but as the condition that makes sustained performance possible.

> *The 3-Bucket architecture is not theoretical to me. It is the financial equivalent of endurance training. You build base. You create buffers. You protect long-term strength from short-term volatility. You design so that one bad season does not undo a decade of discipline.*

Most retirement anxiety is not caused by insufficient wealth. It is caused by the absence of a system. Without a system, every market correction is an existential threat. With a system, a crash is simply a signal to wait.

The 3-Bucket Waterfall

Bucket	Horizon	Purpose	Assets
Bucket 1 Safety	Years 0–4	Liquidity & peace of mind	Govt. bonds, liquid funds, short-duration debt funds

Bucket	Horizon	Purpose	Assets
Bucket 2 Stability	Years 5–12	Medium-term bridge	Balanced funds, income arbitrage
Bucket 3 Growth	Year 13+	Inflation shield & legacy	Equity mutual funds

** For readers familiar with global investment terminology: Bucket 1 corresponds to **Cash equivalents**; Bucket 2 to **Fixed Income / Bonds**; Bucket 3 to **Equities**. The Sanskrit naming, Safety, Stability, Growth, reflects the purpose of each bucket rather than the asset class alone, which is the relevant distinction for the Enough-Point framework.*

The waterfall logic: if equities crash and Bucket 3 loses value, you do not touch it. Buckets 1 and 2 give you a 12-year runway to wait for recovery. You never sell long-term growth assets at a loss under duress.

Bucket 1: Safety : Built Through the Kama Lens

Bucket 1 covers Years 0–4, funded in low-risk, highly liquid assets. It contains three things only:

- **Essential monthly expenditure:** housing, groceries, utilities, healthcare, insurance.
- **Planned Kama expenditures:** the annual holiday, meaningful celebrations; budgeted consciously, experienced without guilt.
- **Emergency buffer:** the quiet cushion that means an unexpected bill does not destabilise the architecture.

What does not belong: status-driven EMIs, unexamined subscriptions, lifestyle inflation that arrived without decision.

Bucket 2: Stability : The Bridge

Bucket 2 covers Years 5–12, in low-risk, medium-term instruments. Its job is patience, not performance. It does not need impressive returns; it needs to be available when Bucket 1 requires replenishment. Without it, the gap between your living expenses and your growth assets would be uncomfortably narrow.

Bucket 3: Growth : The Patient Engine

Bucket 3 is invested entirely in equity mutual funds with one rule: do not touch it for at least 13 years. Most long-term investing fails not because of fund selection but because volatility could not be tolerated without the insulation of Buckets 1 and 2.

> *The market guardrail: if equities crash, do not touch Bucket 3. Your 12-year runway buys patience, and patience is the only true edge available to the long-term investor.*

The Waterfall Replenishment

- **Draw:** each year, live from Bucket 1.
- **Harvest:** once a year, if Bucket 3 has generated gains, harvest them into Bucket 2.
- **Refill:** Bucket 2 flows down to restore Bucket 1's 4-year runway.

If markets have a difficult year, you do not harvest. Bucket 2 absorbs several years of non-replenishment without compromising Bucket 1. You wait. The waterfall resumes.

Why These Numbers? The Logic Behind 4 and 12 Years

When people first encounter the 3-Bucket architecture, two questions arrive immediately. Four years seems short. Twelve years seems long. Both reactions are reasonable and both deserve a direct answer.

The 4-year horizon for Bucket 1 is grounded in the historical behaviour of equity markets. In most documented market downturns, including 2001, 2008, and 2020, equity portfolios recovered their value within 2 to 4 years. A 4-year cash-equivalent runway means that even in a severe downturn, you do not need to touch Bucket 3 at the worst possible time. You wait. The recovery comes to you.

The 12-year combined horizon for Buckets 1 and 2 provides a second layer of insurance. It accounts for the outlier scenario, the extended bear market or extended personal disruption, that falls outside historical norms. Bucket 2's instruments, in moderate-risk, medium-return territory, replenish slowly during bad years and faster during good ones. Together, Buckets 1 and 2 create what an endurance athlete would recognise as a reserve tank:

you may never need it fully, but its presence changes how you run.

Twelve years is not arbitrary. It is the number at which the mathematics of equity recovery and personal life planning intersect comfortably for most working adults. If you build Bucket 3 from age 40, a 13-year non-touch period takes you to 53; well before most retirement timelines. If you build from 50, the architecture still functions, though Bucket 2 carries more weight and requires more capital to fund the longer no-touch window.

> *Four years is not the plan. It is the floor. Twelve years is not the constraint. It is the freedom.*

Inflation Is Not an Afterthought

Every reader of this chapter will ask the same question, whether they say it aloud or not: if my baseline today is ₹75,000 a month, won't inflation mean I need ₹1,00,000 a month in five years? The architecture would be incomplete if it did not answer this directly.

Bucket 1 is not a static vault. It is a living reservoir, replenished annually from the waterfall. Each year, when you calculate what Bucket 1 needs, you calculate at current costs; not the costs from the year the plan was set. If your baseline has risen from ₹75,000 to ₹85,000 due to genuine inflation in essential costs, the Bucket 1 target adjusts accordingly. The architecture is anchored to your real baseline, not a historical one.

Bucket 2 is invested in instruments that are expected to beat inflation over a medium term; balanced funds and income-focused arbitrage. Its job is to bridge the gap between Bucket 1's drawdowns and Bucket 3's long-term growth, and it is sized to do that in real, not nominal, terms.

Bucket 3, equity, is historically the best available long-term hedge against inflation. Over 15-year periods, diversified equity has outpaced inflation in most documented markets by a meaningful margin. It is not a guarantee. It is the best structural tool available to the long-term investor.

The practical implication: when you do your annual waterfall review, you recalculate the Bucket 1 target at current costs. If it has risen due to inflation, the harvest from Bucket 3 absorbs that increase. The architecture adjusts automatically; you do not need to remodel it every year.

> *I understood this most clearly not from a financial model but from watching my father's pension lose ground over twenty years without him ever acknowledging it. The discipline that produced the savings was not connected to any mechanism for protecting their real value over time. The architecture corrects for that. It is the part of the plan he did not have.*

Building the Architecture from Where You Are

The three scenarios earlier in this chapter are illustrations of the architecture fully built. Most readers are not at the destination; they are at various points on the road. The architecture is not only for those who have already arrived. It is designed to be built incrementally, from wherever you are starting.

If you are in your thirties; building the base

Time is your largest asset and the one most easily squandered on consumption that does not serve any of the four Purusharthas. The priority at this stage is not the full 3-Bucket architecture; it is establishing Bucket 1 as a habit before lifestyle inflation fills the available surplus.

Start with three months of your Kama-filtered baseline in a liquid fund. That alone changes your psychological relationship with money. You are no longer one unexpected bill away from anxiety.

From there, build toward six months, then twelve, then the full four years; not in a rush, but as a consistent allocation from each month's surplus.

> *My own twenties were not available for investment. A significant portion of that decade went towards supplementing the household income and meeting basic needs; the kind of starting condition that is familiar to many first-generation professionals from modest families. The first major financial milestone was not a mutual fund. It was a small flat, purchased with partial funding from my father's retirement corpus. That money represented his life savings, and its use meant that my parents, who had spent their entire working lives in rented accommodation, owned a home for the first time, in a quiet suburb of Hyderabad. That was not a financial decision in any conventional sense. It was a Dharma decision. And it was right. The motorcycle that followed*

> *was funded from earnings without a major loan. These were small acts of sufficiency practised before I had language for them.*

The thirties were when structural investment began; a move from bank fixed deposits, whose interest barely covered inflation, into mutual funds. It was a modest start. But it was a start. The Kama filter was applied intuitively rather than formally: children's future was the clear priority, which shaped every other allocation decision that followed.

Bucket 3 should be started early and left entirely alone. A small monthly SIP into a diversified equity fund, started at 32 and untouched until 50, does more work than a large lump sum started at 45. The mathematics of compounding rewards patience over urgency.

If you are in your forties; course-correcting mid-career

The forties are typically the decade when the gap between income and intentionality is widest. Earnings are higher than they have ever been. Lifestyle has expanded to meet them. The surplus that should be building the architecture is instead funding the performance of success.

The Kama filter is most valuable here; not as a theory, but as a practical audit. A mid-career professional who applies the filter honestly often finds ₹20,000 to ₹40,000 of monthly surplus that was previously invisible, because it was being consumed without decision. That recovered surplus is the seed capital for a Bucket 1 that currently does not exist.

The forties are also when Bucket 3 becomes time-sensitive. Starting a non-touch equity position at 42 and holding it to 58 gives a 16-year window; which is the sweet spot for equity compounding. Waiting until 52 halves that runway.

If you are in your fifties or approaching transition

The architecture at this stage is less about building and more about restructuring. The question is not how to grow; it is how to reorganise existing assets into the waterfall sequence before the first drawdown begins.

The Kama filter at this stage often produces its largest impact. A near-retirement professional auditing their genuine baseline against their current expenditure typically finds a 20 to 30 percent reduction available; not through sacrifice, but through the removal of expenditure that accumulated without decision. That reduction directly lowers the capital required to fund the architecture, sometimes dramatically.

> *The question of property ownership sat with me for two decades. For much of my working life I lived in leased accommodation, initially provided by the organisa-*

tions I worked for, later arranged independently. There was always a reason the timing was not right for buying. Mumbai's property market. Career transitions. The years when income was variable and rebuilding took precedence. But beneath those practical reasons was something more honest: I had applied the Kama filter, consciously or not, and my children's education and future security had consistently ranked above the ownership of property in the hierarchy of what genuinely mattered. When I eventually secured a home, it came from a position of sufficiency rather than anxiety. The architecture was in place. The house was a choice, not a relief. That sequence, children first, house later; was not a sacrifice. It was a prioritisation made from clarity about what enough actually meant.

> *The architecture is not a destination you reach after a career. It is a structure you build during one; one layer at a time, from wherever you happen to be standing today.*

Three Scenarios: This Is Not a Rich Man's Game

Scenario A: Salaried Professional; ₹1.5L/month take-home

Monthly take-home	₹1,50,000
Kama-filtered baseline	₹75,000 (after removing ₹25,000 Trishna)
4-year Bucket 1 target	₹36,00,000
Starting point	Fund 12 months first: ₹9,00,000 in liquid funds

Key insight	The Kama filter creates the surplus. The surplus funds the architecture.

Scenario B: Small Business Owner : Variable Income

Average monthly income	₹3,00,000 (range ₹1.5L–₹5L)
Kama-filtered baseline	₹1,20,000
6-year Bucket 1 target	₹86,40,000 (larger to absorb lean periods)
Key insight	Variable income makes the architecture more valuable, not less.

Scenario C: Near-Retirement Executive

Context	Age 58, planning retirement at 62
Kama-filtered baseline	₹2,50,000 (was ₹3,50,000 before Kama filter)
4-year Bucket 1 target	₹1,20,00,000
Key insight	The Kama filter often reduces the capital required significantly.

Scenario C illustration: a baseline of ₹3,50,000 reduced to ₹2,50,000 through the filter. That single adjustment reduces the required Bucket 1 from ₹1,68,00,000 to ₹1,20,00,000; a difference of nearly fifty lakhs, achievable without earning an additional rupee.

The Enough-Point and the 3-Bucket Strategy are not separate frameworks. They are one framework in two parts. Get the Enough-Point right first.

Build the architecture around it. The sequence matters.

✦ Chapter 4 Reflection

1. What is your genuine monthly Bucket 1 number; from your Kama-filtered baseline, not your current expenditure?
2. How many months of that number do you currently have secured in liquid, low-risk assets?
3. What single action this month would move that number in the right direction?

The soul is never born nor dies at any time. It has not come into being, does not come into being, and will not come into being.

— Bhagavad Gita, II.20

CHAPTER 5

The Four Pillars in Balance

Dharma, Artha, Kama, Moksha: A Life Operating System

Every system needs a governing logic. The 3-Bucket Strategy gives you a financial architecture. The Ashta Lakshmi gives you a map of the full wealth landscape. The Kama filter gives you a tool for examining desire. But underneath all of these sits a more fundamental framework; one the Vedic tradition developed not as a financial model but as an operating system for a whole life.

A Lived Correction

By the time I reached my late fifties, I had what my younger self would have considered success; a stable corpus, children educated and charting their own paths. I had the means and, in some ways, the residual habit of wanting to ensure their outcomes. Many parents do; often without realising it. The ambition transfers so naturally, so lovingly, that it feels indistinguishable from care.

> *For many years I believed that financial success had a clear purpose: to ensure that my children could achieve more than I had. Like many parents from modest backgrounds, I carried quiet expectations. I wanted them to pursue the best education. I imagined certain professions for them. I believed that the financial security I had built would help them reach those destinations. Over time I realised something deeper. The real gift of financial security is not control. It is freedom. Each child eventually discovers a path that calls them. That path may not match the expectations of their parents. When financial stability exists, children are able to pursue that calling without fear. That was the moment I understood another*

> *meaning of enough. Enough wealth does not only protect a family. It removes pressure from the next generation to live someone else's dream.*

But sufficiency, properly understood, includes restraint. It includes allowing the next generation the freedom to define their own Dharma; even when your Dharma spent decades funding the conditions that make their choices possible.

> *The Purusharthas are not abstract philosophy to me. They are a lived correction. Artha earned through discipline must not become control. Kama fulfilled must not become projection. Dharma includes knowing when to step back. Moksha begins, sometimes, with releasing expectations; even the noble ones.*

The Four Pillars

Dharma : The Foundation

Dharma is your right way of being in the world; the mode of action aligned with your nature, your responsibilities, and the larger moral order. It is both the ethics of how you earn and the integrity of how you deploy what you earn. Dharma is the pillar most easily sacrificed when the others are under pressure. It is also the one whose absence is felt most acutely when things go quiet.

Artha : The Means

Artha is material prosperity; necessary and legitimate. You cannot fulfil your Dharma without the resources to act. The crucial distinction is between Artha as means and Artha as end. When Artha becomes the end itself, it becomes the golden cage.

> *Artha is not the answer to 'what is a good life?' It is a necessary condition for pursuing that answer. Confusing the condition for the answer is the root of most financial anxiety.*

Kama : The Fullness

Kama represents the legitimate desires and experiences that make a life worth living. Enough Artha enables the fulfilment of Kama. Examined Kama prevents the pursuit of Artha from becoming infinite. Together, they create the conditions in which Moksha, freedom, becomes possible.

Moksha : The Purpose

Moksha means liberation from the compulsive cycle of wanting. The state in which you operate from sufficiency rather than scarcity. A person who has found their Moksha is often more active and purposeful than before; precisely because they are no longer exhausted by the treadmill.

The Purusharthas in Organisational Life

- **Dharma:** Is our growth strategy aligned with our stated values?
- **Artha:** Are we building enough financial resilience to act with integrity when it is costly?
- **Kama:** Which initiatives genuinely serve our purpose, and which are Trishna dressed up as strategy?
- **Moksha:** What is this organisation ultimately for, a decade from now?

The organisations I have seen struggle most are those with sophisticated Artha frameworks and almost no language for Dharma, Kama, or Moksha. Very good at measuring. They have lost the thread of what they are measuring towards.

When the Pillars Conflict

The Purusharthas are not designed to coexist without tension. In a life fully and honestly lived, they will conflict; sometimes sharply. That tension is not a sign that the framework has failed. It is the framework working. The question is not how to eliminate the conflict, but how to navigate it without quietly abandoning one pillar to serve another.

The most common conflict I observed in three decades of corporate life was between Dharma and Artha. The situation presents itself in many forms, but the structure is always the same: you can see clearly what the right thing to do is, and the right thing costs something materially; a relationship, a role, an income stream, a promotion, perhaps even an entire career trajectory.

Consider the procurement leader asked to sign a contract at the insistence of an influential stakeholder, bypassing established due diligence in the name of urgency. Or the executive pressured to make a commitment they know cannot be delivered, because the client relationship is deemed too valuable to risk with uncomfortable honesty. Or the manager asked to quietly implement a restructuring that will harm people unfairly, without raising questions that might slow the decision.

> *In each of these moments, the dilemma is rarely about recognizing what is right. Most people know. The real question is whether one has the capacity to live by that knowledge.*
>
> *For me, the tension was always between Dharma and Artha, and the question behind this was simple: how much Artha do I have in reserve, and does it give me the freedom to act from Dharma right now? It allowed me to accept the material cost of doing what seemed clearly right; a choice made without drama, but not without a consequence.*
>
> *The architecture I describe in this book is therefore not merely about retirement planning. It is about building the financial infrastructure that allows a person to*

> *make decisions from values rather than from desperation.*

The second most common conflict is between Kama and Moksha; between the legitimate pleasures of a good life and the liberation that comes from holding those pleasures lightly. The person who has everything they said they wanted and finds themselves wanting more is not experiencing moral failure. They are experiencing the gap between Kama without examination and the Moksha that examined Kama eventually enables.

The Purusharthas do not resolve these tensions for you. They make them visible. That visibility is the gift. You cannot navigate a conflict you have not named.

> *The pillars will pull against each other. That is not the problem. The problem is when one pillar quietly collapses without a decision being made.*

Which Pillar Have You Been Neglecting?

Most people, if they are honest, have been running on three pillars for years while pretending the fourth is fine.

Dharma is neglected when the career has been driven by income rather than alignment; when the work being done would not be chosen freely if the money were removed from the equation. It announces itself as a specific kind of Sunday-night feeling: a low-grade dread that has nothing to do with the specific tasks of Monday and everything to do with the accumulation of years doing work that does not belong to you.

Artha is neglected when the ideology of minimalism, spiritual detachment, or anti-materialism has been used as a cover for the discomfort of financial planning. Artha is not greed. It is the legitimate material foundation without which Dharma, Kama, and Moksha are theories rather than lived realities. A person who neglects Artha is not spiritually advanced; they are financially fragile.

Kama is neglected when the discipline of accumulation has crowded out the pleasures that accumulation was supposed to enable. The person who has not taken a real holiday in four years because the timing is never right. The person who has deferred the relationship investment until the business is stable. These are not sacrifices. They are withdrawals from the account that funds a life worth living.

Moksha is neglected most often by the highest achievers. The person who has been rewarded for decades for striving does not easily relinquish the identity that striving built. Liberation needs the release of the compulsion to produce, accumulate, and prove; requires a different kind of discipline than the one that got them to the summit. It requires the willingness to ask what the summit was for, and to live with the answer honestly.

The reflection questions at the end of this chapter are designed to identify which pillar has been quietly compromised. The identification is not comfortable. It is necessary.

Finding the Balance

The Purusharthas are not a hierarchy. They are a system of mutual constraints. The Enough-Point is the point at which all four pillars are in sufficient balance that no single one is compromising the others.

> *The goal is not to maximise any single pillar. The goal is to hold all four in a balance that allows each to serve the others.*

✦ Chapter 5 Reflection

1. Which of the four Purusharthas has been quietly neglected in your life, and what specific cost has that had?

2. Describe the last time Dharma and Artha came into direct conflict for you. What did you choose? What would you choose now, with the architecture in place?

3. Are you holding expectations, for yourself or others, that belong to someone else's definition of a good life? Where did those expectations come from, and when did you last examine them?

You have the right to perform your prescribed duties, but you are not entitled to the fruits of your actions.

— Bhagavad Gita, II.47

CHAPTER 6

From Accumulation to Liberation

What Changes When You Have Enough

There is a moment; it does not announce itself loudly; when the architecture is in place, the Enough-Point is defined, and the 12-year runway is funded. It is a quiet moment. And if you have spent decades in accumulation mode, it is also a slightly disorienting one.

The machinery of striving does not switch off automatically. The habits of scarcity have their own momentum. But something has changed. The decisions are different now.

The Disorientation of Arrival

Nobody warns you about this. The books on financial independence describe the destination clearly; freedom from financial anxiety, the ability to choose work on your own terms, the surplus of time that had previously been consumed by the demands of accumulation. What they do not describe is the first year after you get there.

The machinery keeps running. The alert that checks the portfolio at 6am. The reflex calculation of whether the holiday is justifiable. The discomfort with an unstructured afternoon that produces nothing measurable. These are not character flaws. They are the residue of habits built over decades and reinforced daily by the environment of corporate achievement.

> *My own career moved through three distinct phases, each at a different level of financial and psychological readiness. The first two moved between organisations*

> *and industries with ambition intact; always reaching for the next scale, the next complexity, the next validation. The third was different. It came at a point when the honest question was no longer what can I build? but what do I actually want to do, and why? That is not a question ambition answers well. Ambition points forward and upward by design. The third phase required a different navigation instrument; sufficiency. Not contentment in the passive sense, not resignation, but the active recognition that enough had been built, and that the remaining energy deserved to go somewhere chosen rather than somewhere reached for.*

There was a period during the SME years, organisations with variable income, different governance rhythms, less institutional security, when the corpus built during the MNC years was the quiet foundation that made the experimentation possible. The architecture, unnamed at the time but practised through the Kama lens, had done its job. One difficult year did not undo a decade of discipline. I rebuilt slowly and deliberately. The rebuilding was not failure. It was the third transition finding its shape.

> *At sixty, the question that ambition had never asked, what is this actually for, finally had the space to be answered honestly. The answer was not dramatic. It was quiet. It had to do with contribution rather than achievement, with depth rather than scale, with the specific people and problems I was genuinely equipped to serve. That clarity is what the third phase eventually produced. It could not have arrived earlier. It needed the architecture to be in place first. The architecture removes the financial compulsion to strive. It does not remove the habit of striving. That is different work, and it is Chapter 6's real subject.*

The disorientation passes. But it passes faster when you have named it honestly rather than assumed that freedom would feel immediately like freedom.

Identity Beyond the Business Card

There is a dimension of the transition that financial planning almost never addresses. It is not the anxiety of insufficient money. It is the quieter destabilisation of insufficient identity.

For three decades or more, the business card carried the answer to 'who are you?' The title, the organisation, the scale of responsibility, these were not merely professional descriptors. They were the architecture of self. When that architecture is removed, by choice or by circumstance; what remains is not freedom, at first. It is a silence that can feel uncomfortably close to erasure.

This experience is common and almost never discussed honestly. The person who has just left a senior role after thirty years does not easily admit that they feel lost. The language of the transition is expected to be celebratory, finally free, finally time for oneself, but the internal reality is often more ambivalent. The diary is empty. The phone is quieter. The decisions that once arrived with urgency and consequence have stopped arriving. The machinery of identity, like the machinery of striving, does not switch off because the formal role has ended.

> *I found the Vedic concept of Prasada more useful here than any modern framework. Prasada, often translated as grace, or as a divine gift received with gratitude, carries a specific instruction embedded in its meaning: what has been given is to be received openly, not gripped. The career built over three decades is not a score to be defended or improved. It is a Prasada; a gift that arrived through effort and circumstance both, to be used with full engagement and then released without attachment when its season has passed.*

> *That reframing did not eliminate the disorientation. It gave the disorientation a context. The identity built through the corporate years was real and earned. It was also always borrowed; borrowed from a role that was always temporary, always subject to the natural rhythms of a career's arc.*

What replaces it is not nothing. It is something that was always there but crowded out: the self that existed before the title, and the self that can now be expressed without one. The person you are when the business card is put away is not a diminished version of the executive. It is the executive's source, the orientation, the values, the quality of attention, freed from the constraints of a particular role and available for whatever is built next.

> *The business card described what you did. It was never the complete answer to who you are. Prasada asks you to*

> *receive what you have built with gratitude, and then to hold it lightly enough that it can serve rather than define you.*

What Money Cannot Negotiate

When my mother fell ill, I had resources my father never had. Access, treatment, the best medical advice available; the architecture of Artha was in place. And yet there are limits that wealth does not cross. Money can improve odds. It cannot negotiate with impermanence.

> *That experience sharpened something in me. Health is not a line item. Presence is not deferrable. The energy to live fully cannot be postponed to a more convenient decade. Accumulation without attention to vitality is a poor trade. Liberation begins when you understand what money can do, and what it cannot.*

My father saved carefully and did not spend it. My mother's illness reminded me that the time to live from what you have built is not a future reward; it is a present responsibility. The architecture was never the destination. It was always the means.

Career Decisions Made from Purpose, Not Desperation

When even a small Safety Bucket is in place, you develop what I would call a sufficiency posture. You enter negotiations differently. You are able to say no to things that do not align with your values, without the lurch of financial anxiety that previously made no a difficult word.

In over thirty years in corporate leadership, I watched talented people stay in roles that were slowly diminishing them because they could not afford the uncertainty of leaving. The salary had expanded to meet the lifestyle. The lifestyle had expanded to meet the salary. The trap was complete; not through any single decision, but through a thousand small ones made from scarcity.

The architecture changes that arithmetic. It does not guarantee that every career decision will be easy or correct. It guarantees that financial desperation is no longer the primary input. The decision can be made from Dharma; from alignment with what you are actually equipped to do and what the work deserves; rather than from the narrower question of what the bank account requires next month.

> *Operating from sufficiency rather than scarcity allows you to make career decisions based on purpose rather than desperation. That shift is, in itself, a form of Moksha; liberation or freedom.*

Relationships Freed from Financial Anxiety

Financial anxiety is one of the most corrosive forces in family life; not because of the money itself but because of what it does to presence. The person chronically worried about money is managing a background process of calculation and dread that consumes bandwidth that should be available for connection.

The 10,000 Dinners Question; if you only had a finite number of meals left with the people you love, how would you treat this one; is a reminder that Santana Lakshmi, relational wealth, compounds the same way financial wealth does. Every genuinely present dinner is an investment. Every distracted one is a withdrawal.

The Work Is Not Done: It Is Different

Liberation from accumulation does not mean liberation from engagement. The people who navigated this transition most successfully are not people who stopped working. They are people who redirected the energy; from accumulation toward contribution, from growing the pile towards deepening the impact.

The Bhagavad Gita's teaching is precise: act without attachment to the fruits of action. Work with full engagement, complete skill and care. But do not make the outcome the source of your identity or the measure of your worth.

> *True wealth is not about what you gather. It is about who you become and how much of this divine light you allow to shine through your life.*

What Vijaya Lakshmi Actually Looks Like

Vijaya Lakshmi, Impact Wealth, is the dimension that most people understand intellectually and defer practically. It belongs to some future version of themselves who has more time, more stability, more clarity about what contribution looks like. That future version, for most people, never quite arrives.

The architecture removes the primary reason for the deferral. When the financial anxiety is resolved, the bandwidth it consumed becomes available. The question is what to fill it with, and the answer that Vijaya Lakshmi offers is not philanthropic giving or formal mentorship programmes, though those are legitimate expressions of it. It is simpler and more immediate than that.

It is the colleague you could develop if you were not primarily focused on your own next move. The knowledge you could share if you were not protecting it as competitive advantage. The honest opinion you could give if you were not dependent on the relationship's approval for your financial security. The risk you could take on behalf of an idea that matters if you were not running the mental calculation of what failure would cost.

In over thirty years of corporate leadership, I watched the most genuinely impactful people, the ones who left something real behind them in every organisation they touched, operate from a posture that had one thing in common. They were not primarily protecting something. They were primarily contributing something. Their security was internal enough that their energy could move outward.

That posture is not a personality trait. It is a structural condition. The architecture creates it financially. Chapter 5's work on the Purusharthas creates it philosophically. This chapter is the point at which both conditions converge, and Vijaya Lakshmi, the last and largest of the eight dimensions, becomes not an aspiration but a daily practice.

The question shifts from 'how do I protect what I have built?' to 'what do I want to build next, and for whom?' That is not a retirement question. It is an aliveness question. It is available at any age to anyone who has done the work of this book.

> *The architecture was never the destination. It was the condition that makes the destination possible. And the destination is a life from which nothing important has been deferred.*

Secure the runway. Define the enough. Inhabit the life you built. Not accumulate, then live, but accumulate in order to live, and begin living as the accumulation takes shape.

This is what the arc of the book has been moving towards. Enough defined is not a number on a spreadsheet. It is the moment the question stops being asked compulsively and starts being answered honestly. Freedom regained is not retirement; it is the return of bandwidth that was previously consumed by financial anxiety and redirected towards what actually matters. Life rebalanced is not a destination reached once and held. It is the daily practice of attending to all eight dimensions of the Ashta Lakshmi; of holding Dharma, Artha, Kama, and Moksha in honest proportion; of treating the architecture not as a score but as a foundation. The finish line was always yours to define. You have now been given the tools to draw it.

✦ Chapter 6 Reflection

1. When the architecture is in place, what is the first thing you will stop deferring, and what has it cost you to defer it this long?
2. What would Vijaya Lakshmi look like in your specific life, with your specific knowledge and relationships? Not in theory; in practice, next month.
3. Is there something you have been deferring; a health investment, a relationship, a creative pursuit, a contribution; that cannot be recovered if deferred indefinitely?

AFTERWORD

Going Back to Our Roots

A note on ancient wisdom and modern life

I want to be direct about something that might occur to a reader of this book. The frameworks here, the Ashta Lakshmi, the Purusharthas, the concept of Kama as a filter for desire, are drawn from a tradition thousands of years old. And yet they describe the problems of modern life with a precision that contemporary frameworks often do not match.

This is not coincidence. The ancient Indian philosophical tradition was deeply empirical in its approach to human nature. The sages were not primarily theologians. They were observers of human behaviour across lifetimes and generations. The frameworks they developed were tested against experience, refined through practice, and preserved because they worked.

What we have largely discarded in the pursuit of modern efficiency is not the superstition but the wisdom. We kept the productivity frameworks and abandoned the sufficiency frameworks. We kept the goal-setting methodologies and abandoned the question of what the goals were for. We built extraordinary financial models and forgot to ask what the money was supposed to enable.

Going back to our roots is not nostalgia. It is recovery; the recovery of tools set aside not because they stopped working but because we stopped paying attention to the questions they answered.

I am not a scholar of Vedic philosophy. I am a professional who found, at sixty, that the ancient frameworks clarified what the modern ones obscured. I am also a son who watched his father practise sufficiency without ever calling it that, and who watched his mother's illness clarify, with sudden precision, what money can and cannot do.

These are not borrowed insights. They are earned ones.

Ask the question nobody asks. Sit with it until you have an honest answer. Build accordingly. And then live from what you built.

Sreedhar K

March 2026

GLOSSARY OF WISDOM

Key terms from the Vedic tradition used in this book, with their modern applications.

Adi Lakshmi

The primordial form of Lakshmi representing the source of all wealth; internal, spiritual, and foundational. In this book, the dimension of spiritual and inner wealth: the morning practice, the stillness that precedes the day.

Artha

One of the four Purusharthas. Material prosperity, wealth, and worldly security. Legitimate and necessary, but as a means to a fuller life, never as an end in itself.

Ashta Lakshmi

The eight forms of Lakshmi, the goddess of prosperity. Each represents a distinct dimension of wealth: spiritual, financial, health, social, relational, courage, intellectual, and impact. Together they define the full landscape of a prosperous life.

Bhagavad Gita

A 700-verse Hindu scripture that forms part of the Mahabharata. A dialogue between the prince Arjuna and the god Krishna on the eve of battle; addressing duty, righteousness, action, and the nature of the self.

Bhoga

The dimension of Kama representing legitimate enjoyment and pleasure. Distinguished from Trishna by intention: Bhoga is chosen deliberately, anticipated, and experienced without guilt.

Dhairya Lakshmi

The Lakshmi of courage, valour, and patience. In this book, Psychological Wealth; the inner reserve that enables reinvention, risk-taking, and perseverance under uncertainty.

Dhana Lakshmi

The Lakshmi of financial wealth. Understood in this book not as an end but as fuel for freedom; the means to act with purpose and say no to misalignment.

Dhanya Lakshmi

The Lakshmi of nourishment, grains, and health. In this book, Health Wealth; the energy levels, physical vitality, and longevity that make all other pursuits possible.

Dharma

One of the four Purusharthas. One's right way of being in the world; aligned with nature, responsibility, and the moral order. The ethical foundation upon which all other goals rest.

Enough-Point

The author's central concept. The honest, Kama-filtered threshold of expenditure at which a life can be lived fully without the anxiety of scarcity. Not the minimum one can endure, but the optimum one can define.

Gaja Lakshmi

The Lakshmi of elephants; symbols of royalty, loyalty, and social intelligence. In this book, Social Wealth: the network, reputation, and community that support and are supported by your life's work.

Kama

One of the four Purusharthas. Conscious, bounded desire; the legitimate pleasures, experiences, and connections that make a life worth living. Distinguished from Trishna (unexamined craving) by the presence of intention and examination.

Moksha

One of the four Purusharthas. Liberation; freedom from the compulsive cycle of wanting and accumulating. Not passivity, but purposeful action freed from the anxiety that corrupts striving.

Purusharthas

The four aims of human life in the Hindu tradition: Dharma (right action), Artha (material prosperity), Kama (conscious desire), and Moksha (liberation). Together, they form a complete operating system for a meaningful life.

Rati

The dimension of Kama associated with love, connection, and deep relationship. In this book, the reminder that the deepest needs require time more than money.

Santana Lakshmi

The Lakshmi of family, progeny, and relational legacy. In this book, Relational Wealth; the quality of close relationships, the presence offered to those we love, and the legacy built within the family.

Trishna

Unexamined craving; desire that has not been tested, questioned, or consciously chosen. In this book, the Vedic name for lifestyle creep and the mechanism of the hedonic treadmill.

Upakarana

The dimension of Kama representing legitimate comforts and material supports. Defined by function rather than ego: the healthcare, workspace, and tools that enable dignity, productivity, and health.

Vidya Lakshmi

The Lakshmi of knowledge, wisdom, and education. In this book, Intellectual Wealth; the continuous pursuit of mastery, the curiosity that keeps the mind alive at any age.

Vijaya Lakshmi

The Lakshmi of victory and overcoming obstacles. In this book, Impact Wealth; the victory of a life lived for something larger than oneself, measured in lives touched and positive change catalysed.

THE ENOUGH TOOLKIT

A Practical Appendix

This toolkit translates the book's frameworks into three working exercises. Use them in sequence, returning to each one as your circumstances change.

Exercise 1 : The Ashta Lakshmi Audit

Score yourself honestly 1–10 on each dimension. Then answer the three questions below.

Dimension	Modern Lens	Your Score (1–10)
Adi Lakshmi	Spiritual / Internal Wealth	___
Dhana Lakshmi	Financial Wealth	___

Dimension	Modern Lens	Your Score (1–10)
Dhanya Lakshmi	Health Wealth	___
Gaja Lakshmi	Social Wealth	___
Santana Lakshmi	Relational / Family Wealth	___
Dhairya Lakshmi	Psychological / Courage Wealth	___
Vidya Lakshmi	Intellectual Wealth	___
Vijaya Lakshmi	Impact / Service Wealth	___

Your three audit questions:

Question	Your Answer
Where is the largest gap between financial wealth and the rest?	
Which dimension, if improved, would most change your daily experience?	
What trade have you made, conscious or not, between dimensions?	

Exercise 2; The Kama Filter

Take your last three months of bank and card statements. For each significant expenditure, complete the table below. Be honest; this exercise is for you, not for an audience.

Expenditure / Category	Monthly Amount	Kama Dimension	Keep / Remove / Reduce

Expenditure / Category	Monthly Amount	Kama Dimension	Keep / Remove / Reduce

Kama Dimension guide: B = Bhoga (planned pleasure) · T = Trishna (unexamined craving) · R = Rati (connection) · U = Upakarana (functional comfort)

Exercise 3 : Your 3-Bucket Planner

Complete this planner after applying the Kama filter. Use your honest monthly baseline, not your current expenditure.

Item	Question / Prompt	Your Number / Answer
Honest monthly baseline	*After the Kama filter; what does your life genuinely cost?*	
Annual baseline	*Monthly × 12*	
Bucket 1 target	*Annual baseline × 4 years*	
Current Bucket 1	*Liquid funds + cash + short-term bonds today*	
Bucket 1 gap	*Target minus current*	
Monthly surplus	*Income minus Kama-filtered baseline*	

Item	**Question / Prompt**	**Your Number / Answer**
Months to close gap	*Gap divided by monthly surplus*	
Bucket 2 target	*Annual baseline × 8 years*	
Bucket 3 status	*Equity investments not to be touched for 13+ years*	
First action this month	*One specific step toward Bucket 1*	

The architecture does not guarantee a perfect life. It guarantees a life where financial fear stops driving your decisions.

ABOUT THE AUTHOR

Sreedhar K spent over thirty years at the intersection of strategy and execution in global organisations; leading transformations in procurement, supply chain, and operations across industries and geographies. He worked at the leadership level in some of the world's most demanding corporate environments, where he observed, at close range, the patterns of accumulation and the questions that accumulation consistently failed to answer.

Closer to sixty, he made a deliberate transition to independent advisory work; a move made possible, he would say, not primarily by financial calculation, but by having defined his Enough-Point. The frameworks in this book were not developed for the page. They were lived before they were written.

Alongside his corporate career, Sreedhar pursued endurance sport with the same discipline he brought to his professional life. He has completed half marathons, 200km cycling brevets, open-water swims, and 70.3 Iron-distance triathlons. The endurance athlete's relationship with pacing, reserves, and the difference between short-term pain and long-term structure runs through everything in this book, even when it is not named.

He is a student of Vedic philosophy; not as a scholar, but as a practitioner who found, at sixty, that the ancient frameworks answered questions that three decades of excellent modern planning had left open.

He is the eldest son of parents who taught him, without a single word about money, everything that matters most about wealth. This book is, in part, their legacy.

This is his first book.

ACKNOWLEDGEMENTS

Every book is a collaboration, even the ones written in solitude.

To my father, who never read a book on personal finance but understood its most important principle better than anyone I have met since: that the size of the blanket sets the terms, and that dignity lies in adjusting accordingly rather than borrowing the difference.

To my mother, whose illness taught me what no corporate career could; the precise boundary between what Artha can do and what it cannot. That lesson is in these pages, briefly but honestly.

To the colleagues, leaders, and peers who allowed me to observe their careers at close range over three decades. The patterns in this book, the trap, the treadmill, the comparison, the difficult transitions, are drawn from what I watched alongside you. No names, but you will recognise what I saw.

To the clients and leaders, I have worked with in advisory practice, who asked questions I had not yet articulated and pushed me toward answers I did not expect to find. Every good consulting engagement teaches the consultant more than the client.

To the early readers of the manuscript; the friends who knew my life well enough to tell me when the personal thread did not ring closer to lived experience, and the professional colleagues who told me when the frameworks needed to do more work. Your honesty was the most useful gift.

To the ancient tradition that produced the Ashta Lakshmi, the Purusharthas, and the Bhagavad Gita; whose authors I cannot name but whose observations I have found more accurate about the human condition than most of what has been written in the centuries since.

And to anyone reading this who has spent years answering what and how and has not yet found a framework for why; this book was written for you.

Disclaimer: This content is for informational and educational purposes only and does not constitute financial, investment, or legal advice. Consult with a qualified professional before making significant financial decisions.

www.ingramcontent.com/pod-product-compliance
Lightning Source LLC
Chambersburg PA
CBHW062110160726
48282CB00026B/735
9789357868242